ALTERNATOR BOOKS™

SPACE IN ACTION

COMETS AND ASTEROIDS IN ACTION

An AUGMENTED REALITY Experience

T0385088

Kevin Kurtz

Lerner Publications ◆ Minneapolis

EXPLORE SPACE IN BRAND-NEW WAYS WITH AUGMENTED REALITY!

1. Ask a parent or guardian for permission to download the free Lerner AR app on your digital device by going to the App Store or Google Play.

2. As you read, look for this icon throughout the book. It means there is an augmented reality experience on that page!

3. Use the Lerner AR app to scan the picture near the icon.

4. Watch space come alive with augmented reality!

CONTENTS

INTRODUCTION

EXPLOSION IN THE SKY

In 1908 a man in Siberia, Russia, was knocked out of his chair by an exploding asteroid. It detonated 40 miles (64 km) away, but the blast had enough force to throw him off his porch. Its heat made him feel as if he was on fire. He felt the ground tremble. When he looked up, the sky seemed to be in flames.

The 1908 asteroid explosion in Russia flattened eighty million trees.

The asteroid exploded over a remote part of Russia, killing hundreds of reindeer and other animals but causing few injuries to humans.

The 220-million-pound (100 million kg) asteroid traveled at about 33,500 miles (53,913 km) per hour. As the chunk of rock and metal burned up in Earth's atmosphere, **friction** heated the air around it to 44,500°F (24,704°C). The heat and increasing air pressure from the atmosphere caused the asteroid to explode.

The blast, named the Tunguska event after a nearby river, may have been the first asteroid explosion witnessed by humans. And because the solar system is full of comets and asteroids, it probably won't be the last.

CHAPTER 1

MEET YOUR NEIGHBORS

In 1910 a glowing ball with a long, sparkling tail appeared in the sky. Halley's comet was passing near Earth. Some people thought gas from the comet would kill people. A few businesses started making anti-comet pills, which promised to protect people from this deadly gas.

Halley's comet is named after Edmond Halley, the first scientist to predict the comet's seventy-six-year cycle. He was proven right in 1758, sixteen years after his death.

The *Rosetta* spacecraft captured this image of a comet's surface in 2016. Comets have more ice than asteroids have.

The comet soon passed by without hurting anyone. Halley's comet has been streaking near Earth for thousands of years. About every seventy-six years, the comet can be observed in the sky during its long **orbit** around the sun. It's just one of more than a trillion comets and asteroids in our solar system.

This image shows the relative sizes of the asteroid Vesta (*left*), the dwarf planet Ceres (*middle*), and Earth's moon.

WHAT ARE COMETS AND ASTEROIDS?

Asteroids and comets are objects in space that are smaller than planets. Asteroids are mainly rock and metal. Many asteroids, such as Kleopatra, have irregular, lumpy shapes. Some, such as Vesta, are round. Most asteroids in the solar system orbit the sun between Mars and Jupiter, in the asteroid belt.

Comets are frozen balls of dust and ice. Some comets pass near the sun. When this happens, the comet heats up and forms a glowing tail of gas and dust that can be millions of miles long. Comets can be bright enough to see from Earth without a telescope.

Comets become more active and visible as they approach perihelion, their closest position to the sun.

The solar system's comets are found mostly in the Kuiper Belt and the Oort Cloud. The Kuiper Belt is a band of comets and icy objects located past Neptune. Dwarf planet Pluto is in the Kuiper Belt.

Pluto is about forty times farther from the sun than Earth is. The dwarf planet orbits the sun once every 248 Earth years.

The solar system has trillions of asteroids and comets in the asteroid belt, Kuiper Belt, and Oort Cloud.

The Oort Cloud is even farther from the sun. Comets there are more than 93 billion miles (150 billion km) from the center of the solar system. Scientists think more than one trillion comets orbit in the Oort Cloud.

CHAPTER 2

DINOSAUR KILLER

In 2016 scientists on a boat in the Gulf of Mexico drilled into an **impact crater** buried under the seafloor. An asteroid or comet created the crater by crashing into Earth sixty-six million years ago. The impact started a chain of events that most likely led to the extinction of dinosaurs and about 76 percent of all plant and animal species on Earth. Scientists studied rocks from the crater to learn more about what happens when a massive asteroid or comet strikes Earth.

Rocks from the impact crater in the Gulf of Mexico, such as this one, can tell scientists about the size, speed, and destructive power of the asteroid or comet.

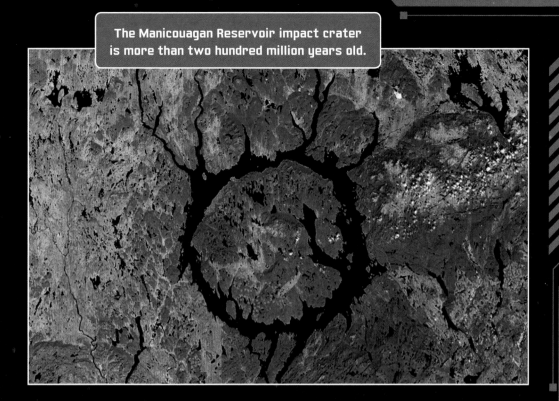

An impact crater is created by an asteroid or comet crashing into a larger object. Scientists have discovered fewer than two hundred impact craters on Earth. Some are easy to see, such as the Manicouagan Reservoir in Quebec, Canada. Others are hidden underground or deep in the ocean. **Erosion** and glaciers likely destroyed many of Earth's craters.

There are millions of observable impact craters on the moon. The moon doesn't have an atmosphere to protect it from impacts. It also doesn't have forces of erosion such as wind and water, allowing craters to last much longer than they do on Earth.

Chicxulub crater may have looked like this not long after it was created.

The crater in the Gulf of Mexico, Chicxulub crater, is one of the best-preserved impact craters on Earth. It is buried under sixty-six million years of **sediment** and rock. The sediment and rock protect the crater from erosion.

Scientists think the Chicxulub object was about 7.5 miles (12 km) wide. It may have been traveling 40,000 miles (64,373 km) per hour when it struck Earth. The impact caused rock to splash like water and created the 124-mile-wide (200 km) crater.

An artist's impression shows how the Chicxulub impact may have looked from space.

A BAD DAY FOR DINOSAURS

The Chicxulub impact had the force of one billion atomic bombs. Every living thing within hundreds of miles died instantly.

The impact threw enough dust into Earth's atmosphere to block the sun for years.

An artist's impression of the
Chicxulub crater from space

    The asteroid crashed in a shallow ocean, creating **tsunamis**
up to 5,000 feet (1,524 m) high. The impact set off massive
earthquakes around the world. Dust blown into the air blocked
out the sun. Plants and animals couldn't survive without
sunlight, leading to **mass extinction**.

CHAPTER 3

WANDERERS FROM FAR AWAY

People might have seen a red glow in the night sky seventy thousand years ago. The light came from Scholz's star, a **red dwarf**. Scholz's star was passing through our solar system. It is now about 20 **light-years** from Earth.

Scientists think red dwarfs are the most common stars in the galaxy. Most of them are too dim to see from Earth without a telescope.

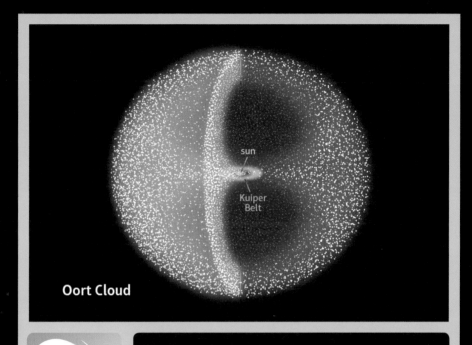

Oort Cloud

sun

Kuiper Belt

Astronomers believe that the Oort Cloud is like a giant shell that surrounds the rest of the solar system.

As Scholz's star traveled through the solar system, it may have invaded the Oort Cloud. By studying the orbits of comets that pass near the sun, **astronomers** learned that some of them came from the same region of the Oort Cloud that Scholz's star likely passed through. The red dwarf could have knocked comets out of the cloud, changing their orbit and sending them hurtling toward the sun and Earth. Passing objects such as Scholz's star could explain why Halley's comet and others follow unusual orbits that bring them near Earth.

INTERSTELLAR INVADER

In 2017 astronomers noticed a strange object hurtling past the orbit of Mars. The object, named Oumuamua, was shaped more like a blue whale or a cucumber than a typical asteroid or comet. It moved faster than most objects and traveled in an unexpected direction. At first, astronomers weren't sure what Oumuamua was. It was so unusual that some thought it might be a **probe** sent by aliens.

This telescope in Arizona is part of the Catalina Sky Survey, a project that searches space for objects such as Oumuamua.

Astronomers had never observed a comet or asteroid in our solar system that was as long and skinny as Oumuamua was.

After studying Oumuamua, most scientists think it is a weirdly shaped comet. It likely came from another solar system billions of miles away. That's why its speed and direction are different from other objects in the solar system.

This makes Oumuamua the first alien asteroid or comet from outside our solar system observed by astronomers. Yet these visits may be common. A few months after Oumuamua's discovery, scientists observed an asteroid near Jupiter that is also from another solar system.

CHAPTER 4

VISITING COMETS AND ASTEROIDS

O n September 30, 2016, a spacecraft crashed on a comet. *Rosetta* had been orbiting comet 67P/Churyumov-Gerasimenko on its path around the sun.

The comet and *Rosetta* were traveling away from the sun near the orbit of Jupiter. The spacecraft ran on solar energy, and soon it would be too far from the sun to keep working. So mission controllers on Earth decided to crash it into the comet before losing it forever. *Rosetta* captured photos and information about 67P/Churyumov-Gerasimenko as it fell to the comet's surface.

Comet 67P/Churyumov-Gerasimenko is lumpy and looks like two objects stuck together.

KEYS TO THE PAST

The solar system started as a cloud of gas and dust. Over time, the gas and dust joined together to form the sun, planets, comets, asteroids, and more. Comets and asteroids don't experience erosion, so they change very little over time. Studying them allows scientists to learn more about our early solar system.

Early Solar System

Asteroids and comets that formed when the solar system was young haven't changed much since then.

To explore the interior of comets, NASA's *Deep Impact* crashed a probe into a comet in 2005. Another spacecraft, NASA's *OSIRIS-REx*, is currently studying asteroid Bennu. *OSIRIS-REx* will collect a sample from Bennu and bring it to Earth in 2023. The sample will provide clues about what the early solar system was like.

OSIRIS-REx will collect a sample from Bennu, map the asteroid's surface, and study its orbit.

This illustration shows a missile streaking toward an asteroid. The missile will explode near the asteroid to change its direction.

STOPPING THE NEXT IMPACT

Events as destructive as the Chicxulub impact are rare. Yet it's possible another big object could strike Earth. NASA is making plans to prevent this. The space agency could knock an asteroid or comet off course by ramming it with a heavy object or by exploding a nuclear bomb near it. The force of the impact or explosion might push the object away from Earth.

NASA's Planetary Defense Coordination Office tracks potentially dangerous objects in space. They have observed only one comet or asteroid that has a chance to hit us in the future. Asteroid Bennu has a one in twenty-seven hundred chance of striking Earth on September 22, 2135.

Bennu is about 0.3 miles (0.5 km) wide in the middle, slightly wider than the height of New York's Empire State Building.

Soon after it formed, Earth's atmosphere was thinner than it is now, allowing more asteroids and comets to impact the surface.

Comets and asteroids carry water and other essential ingredients for life. Long ago, they carried these ingredients to Earth. Some scientists think life wouldn't have started here without comet and asteroid impacts. The Chicxulub impact and the extinction of dinosaurs led to the rise of mammals, and eventually humans. By studying comets and asteroids, we learn more about our solar system as well as ourselves.

Follow the URLs below to download 3D printer design files for *Rosetta* and two of the asteroids in this book:

Bennu, http://qrs.lernerbooks.com/Bennu

Kleopatra, http://qrs.lernerbooks.com/Kleopatra

Rosetta, http://qrs.lernerbooks.com/Rosetta

astronomers: scientists who study objects and events in space

erosion: to wear away by wind, water, or ice

friction: the force created by two objects rubbing against each other

impact crater: a bowl-shaped hole created by an asteroid or comet smashing into a larger object

light-years: units of measurement equal to the distance light can travel in one year

mass extinction: when a large number of plant and animal species cease to exist in a relatively short period of time

orbit: the path around a body in space, or to move around that path

probe: a machine that explores an object in space

red dwarf: a common type of star with a relatively low temperature

sediment: matter such as sand and the remains of animals that builds up on the seafloor over time

tsunamis: huge waves caused by events such as earthquakes or landslides

FURTHER INFORMATION

Asteroids—The Minor Planets
https://www.esa.int/kids/en/learn/Our_Universe/Comets_and
_meteors/

Comet Facts for Kids
http://www.sciencekids.co.nz/sciencefacts/space/comets.html

Dickmann, Nancy. *Exploring Comets, Asteroids, and Other Objects in Space.* New York: Rosen, 2016.

Kenney, Karen Latchana. *Breakthroughs in Planet and Comet Research.* Minneapolis: Lerner Publications, 2019.

NASA Space Place—Solar System
https://spaceplace.nasa.gov/menu/solar-system/

National Geographic Kids—Asteroids
https://kids.nationalgeographic.com/explore/space/asteroids
/#asteroid-belt.jpg

Rathburn, Betsy. *Comets.* Minneapolis: Bellwether Media, 2019.

Rusch, Elizabeth. *Impact!: Asteroids and the Science of Saving the World.* Boston: Houghton Mifflin Harcourt, 2017.

Photo Acknowledgments

Image credits: Freer/Shutterstock.com, p. 2 (bottom); Sovfoto/Universal Images Group/Getty Images, p. 4; muratart/Shutterstock.com, p. 5; NASA, p. 6; ESA/Rosetta/MPS for OSIRIS Team MPS/UPD/LAM/IAA/SSO/INTA/UPM/DASP/IDA, p. 7; Moon image: Gregory H. Revera, Ceres image: Justin Cowart, Vesta image: NASA/JPL-Caltech/UCAL/MPS/DLR/IDA (CC BY-SA 3.0), p. 8; G. Hüdepohl (atacamaphoto.com)/ESO, p. 9; NASA/Johns Hopkins University Applied Physics Laboratory/Southwest Research Institute, p. 10; BSIP/UIG/Getty Images, p. 11; Kike Calvo/Universal Images Group/Getty Images, p. 12; ESA, p. 13; Detlev van Ravenswaay/Science Source, p. 14; D. VAN RAVENSWAAY/Science Photo Library/Getty Images, p. 15; NASA/Donald E. Davis, p. 16; MARK GARLICK/SCIENCE PHOTO LIBRARY/Getty Images, p. 17; dotted zebra/Alamy Stock Photo, p. 18; Laura Westlund/Independent Picture Service, p. 19; John Davis/Stocktrek Images/Getty Images, p. 20; ESO/M. Kornmesser, p. 21; ESA/Rosetta/NAVCAM (CC BY-SA IGO 3.0), p. 22; NASA/Goddard Space Flight Center, p. 24; SCIEPRO/Science Photo Library/Getty Images, p. 25; NASA/Goddard/University of Arizona/Lockheed Martin, p. 26; Mark Stevenson/UIG/Getty Images, p. 27; Chumphon Whangchom/EyeEmy/Getty Images, p. 28. Design elements: Jetrel/Shutterstock.com; Nanashiro/Shutterstock.com; phiseksit/Shutterstock.com; MSSA/Shutterstock.com; Pakpoom Makpan/Shutterstock.com; pixelparticle/Shutterstock.com; wacomka/Shutterstock.com; fluidworkshop/Shutterstock.com.

Cover: sdecoret/Shutterstock.com; muratart/Shutterstock.com (design element).

Lerner Publications Company
An imprint of Lerner Publishing Group, Inc.
241 First Avenue North
Minneapolis, MN 54001 USA

For reading levels and more information, look up this title at www.lernerbooks.com.

Main body text set in Aptifer Sans LT Pro.
Typeface provided by Linotype AG.

Library of Congress Cataloging-in-Publication Data

Names: Kurtz, Kevin, author.
Title: Comets and asteroids in action : an augmented reality experience / Kevin Kurtz.
Description: Minneapolis : Lerner Publications, [2020] | Series: Space exploration (Alternator Books) | Audience: Ages 8–12. | Audience: Grades 4 to 6. | Includes bibliographical references and index.
Identifiers: LCCN 2019016702 (print) | LCCN 2019019824 (ebook) | ISBN 9781541583474 (eb pdf) | ISBN 9781541578852 (lb : alk. paper) | ISBN 9781541589421 (pb : alk. paper)
Subjects: LCSH: Asteroids—Juvenile literature. | Comets—Juvenile literature.
Classification: LCC QB651 (ebook) | LCC QB651 .K855 2020 (print) | DDC 523.44—dc23

LC record available at https://lccn.loc.gov/2019016702

Manufactured in the United States of America
1-46988-47857-7/30/2019